Praise for *Leadership Secrets of Santa Claus*

"I've always loved Santa Claus—and now that I know his leadership secrets, I love him even more! Read this book and learn how returning to your childhood can make you a better adult—and a better leader."
—Ken Blanchard
New York Times bestselling author of *The One Minute Manager*

"This warm, wonderful book is loaded with great ideas for leaders at all levels to build a peak performing team of highly motivated people."
—Brian Tracy
New York Times bestselling author, speaker

"Forget the naughty. *The Leadership Secrets of Santa Claus* makes the nicest gift for any leader in your life—not just at Christmastime, but all year long! It offers a creative twist on some sage business advice that too often gets forgotten. If you want a reward for being good—*this is it*!"
—Dr. Bob Nelson
Bestselling author of *1501 Ways to Reward Employees*

"*The Leadership Secrets of Santa Claus* will have your workshop running smoother, your elves happier, and your business thriving, not just during the holidays, but all year long. I think it's destined to be a classic for years to come!"
—Vic Conant
CEO Nightingale-Conant Corporation

"*The Leadership Secrets of Santa Claus* delivers classic leadership lessons in an entertaining style. With the best lessons on how to keep your business running smoothly all year round, this book is a must-read for every leader, at any time of year."
—Stedman Graham
Bestselling author, speaker, entrepreneur

"This is a brilliant book with solid substance on transformational leadership. A great read."
—Nido Qubein
President of High Point University,
Chairman Great Harvest Bread Co.

"*The Leadership Secrets of Santa Claus* is a rare gem. It's filled with tools that any leader can put in effect TODAY to change the productivity and effectiveness of their own workplace, but it's told in such an engaging way that you won't want to put it down."
—Andy Andrews
New York Times bestselling author of *The Noticer* and *The Traveler's Gift*

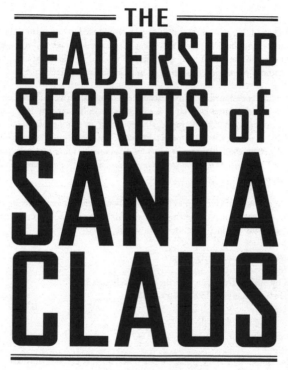

THE LEADERSHIP SECRETS of SANTA CLAUS

ERIC HARVEY

simple truths
LEAD TO CHANGE

an imprint of Sourcebooks, Inc.

Published by Simple Truths, an imprint of Sourcebooks, Inc.
P.O. Box 4410, Naperville, Illinois 60567-4410
(630) 961-3900
Fax: (630) 961-2168
www.sourcebooks.com

Originally published in 2003 in the United States of America by Performance
Systems Corporation.

Printed and bound in the United States of America.
WOZ 10 9 8 7 6 5 4 3 2 1

Additional Simple Truths of Business

Change Is Good...You Go First
Bull's-Eye
You Can't Send a Duck to Eagle School

A SACKFUL OF CONTENTS

SANTA'S HELPERS

David Cottrell *and* **Al Lucia** *have helped hundreds of organizations, and their leaders, build high-performance workplaces with motivated coworkers. Their work is based on the belief that effective leaders accomplish "big things" by* **giving** *employees clear goals, solid accountabilities, and ongoing feedback, coaching, and recognition. These are the leadership traits of the Santa Claus in each of us. Special thanks to our creative "head elf"* **Steve Ventura** *for helping us get this big thing done.*

INTRODUCTION
It's not easy being Santa Claus!

Believe you me, having to smile and be jolly every day when you're wearing the same thick, hot, red wool suit (that itches like crazy) is no picnic.

This is a job that will definitely strain your sanity and drain your ego if you let it. Seems like everyone wants a piece of me. Yet many of the people I serve question my existence…or just plain don't believe in me at all. And those who *do* believe often expect me to do the impossible—rarely caring about what I have to do, or go through (including chimneys), to meet their expectations. And they *ALL* have expectations.

Give people exactly what they want, and Ho, Ho, Ho—everybody loves good Ol' Santa. But miss one or two items on the list—or forget to include the batteries—and you'd better be ready for the alligator tears, the fat jokes, the stupid songs, no cookies, the wet laps, the yanks on the beard, and the "I could do Santa's job better than Santa" remarks. And that's only half of why it's not easy being me.

There's no doubt that my biggest challenges come from two roles that people rarely associate with this red-cheeked, bag-carrying sleigh driver: Santa the *MANAGER* and Santa the *LEADER*.

I am, after all, running a business here. I'm a boss. I've got responsibilities—both to the gift-*getters* and the gift-*makers*. There are workers to lead, letters to read, orders to fill, processes to manage, stuff to buy, stuff to make, standards to maintain, new technologies to adopt, skills to develop, elf problems to solve, and reindeer droppings to scoop (although I delegate that one). Trust me, I've got some big boots to fill.

It's true that over the centuries I've learned a lot from mistakes and miscalculations. One year, for example, my well-planned toy production schedule was thrown completely out of whack by last-minute changes in customer requirements. I thought I had a good read on what the kiddies were wanting, and we had geared up for a big push on dolls and board games. Then a new movie came out and *WHAM*—all of a sudden everyone now wanted *computer* and *video* games based on the movie. Boy did we do some last-minute scrambling! We were working 24–7 to deal with that one. What a production challenge! What a motivation challenge!

Another year, I had two reindeer come down with the flu right after Prancer pulled the plug, retired, and took off for Florida. That left me with a 33 percent delivery staff reduction (if you count Rudolph) with no immediate replacements. And the number of houses to visit had increased by 17 percent. Talk about "doing more with less"! That year was not only tough on me, but also placed an extra load on the rest of the reindeer. Those puppies were really dragging by the time we finished at the last house. We barely made it back. They were ticked and I was tired. But since it takes almost a year to train new harness-team members, there was no rest to be enjoyed. I had to immediately post the open positions and start reviewing reindeer résumés.

Like most managers, I have to deal with marketplace fluctuations ("Dear Santa, I thought I wanted *that*, but now I want *this*."). And I've seen more than my share of budget cuts, staff reductions, employees who are either unwilling or unable to adjust to change, technology advancements, increasing demands for higher quality and better service, fluctuations in the economy, competing priorities, ever-growing performance expectations (for all of us), and a whole lot more. Whew!

Think your job is tough? *You* try recruiting in, and for, the North Pole; *you* try retooling your plant—and retraining your people—every year to produce the newest fads in toys; *you* try delivering tons of presents on a route as big as mine—all in one long night.

No, it's not easy being Santa Claus. But in spite of that, **I love what I do.** People need me—they depend on me. We're doing something important here. And knowing that gives me the energy to carry the sack, lead the pack, and keep coming back.

By now, you may be wondering how I meet all of these challenges and responsibilities…how I manage to bring everyone and everything together to complete our mission. Some people think I use magic. But really, there's no magic about it.

Introduction

So, if it's not magic, what *is* my secret? Actually there are ten of them—ten practical strategies for leading others and getting big things done all year long. They're called "The Leadership Secrets of Santa Claus," and I'm here to share them *with* you.

They are my gifts *to* you. And I guarantee that if you apply them, you'll find these "secrets" more valuable than anything you might have written on your holiday wish list.

Read on! Lead on!

Santa Claus

BUILD A WONDERFUL WORKSHOP

Make the Mission the Main Thing

When it comes to getting "big things" done well, there are few (if any) businesses that can hold a Yule candle to our North Pole operation. I'm extremely proud of the workshop that the elves, reindeer, and I have created—and we're more than happy to show it off. But, at ninety degrees north latitude and minus fifty degrees Fahrenheit, we get very few takers on our standing offer to tour the facility. Most southerners (everyone's a southerner to us) only see our plant through their imaginations…through the stereotypical images they've had of Santa's Workshop since childhood.

What's your vision of our workplace? Do you see candy canes and chestnuts? Wood chips flying in the air and falling into neat little piles? Whistling and singing? Busy little elves and reindeer, with smiles on their faces, scurrying around to make and package toys? If so, your image is right on—except for the candy canes and chestnuts...and the wood chips (we rarely use wood any more).

Yes, we do run a productive and happy place here. And that's in spite of the intense pressures and challenges we face—ones that undoubtedly were *not* included in your vision of us. So how do we do it? Just how do *I* keep everyone, including myself, on track and motivated throughout each year—all for one long night's big splash? The answer is basic and simple: through an unwavering and uncompromising focus on *OUR MISSION*. And as the leader, I've taken several steps to establish and maintain that focus.

First, I've made sure that all the elves and reindeer know what our mission is ("Making spirits bright by building and delivering high-quality toys to good little girls and boys") and why it's important. Ask any member of our North Pole staff and they can quote our mission verbatim...*and* explain its significance.

Second, I've spent time with individual employees—discussing how their respective jobs specifically link with, and contribute to, the accomplishment of our mission.

Third, I've kept the mission "in front of folks" by posting it on walls, discussing it at staff meetings and training sessions, including it in internal correspondence, and through a host of other activities that help ensure it stays our central focal point.

Finally, I've made it a core component of our decision-making and work-planning processes. If an action we're considering doesn't support our mission, either directly or indirectly, we don't do it!

With all the team members we have, orders we get, toys we make, and issues we face, it could be way too easy to dilute ourselves, head off on tangents, or just plain lose sight of why we're here. We avoid those by keeping our mission at the heart of everything we do…by making our mission our main thing. I recommend that you do the same in *your* workshop.

Focus on Your People As Well As Your Purpose

Here's a nugget of leadership wisdom that I've picked up over the decades—something you can take to one of the toy banks we occasionally deliver: you can't possibly focus on your mission without also focusing on the folks that make your mission happen. The two go hand in hand…hoof in hoof (sorry, but the reindeer insisted). And besides, since you manage *things* and lead *people*, common sense suggests that it's *people* who are at the core of all leadership activities.

But alas, common sense apparently isn't all that common. There is a handful of managers out there who don't get it—they don't get the message, and they don't get the positive results that the message can help produce. That point was clearly brought home by a short letter I received several years ago:

> Dear Santa:
> This year I only want one thing—a manager who cares as much about me as the work I'm doing. It's hard to be committed when there's no reciprocation. Please help!

Now that's a sad commentary…and a tall order to fill. There was no need to check our production schedule. I already knew that "caring leaders" weren't on our list of deliverables. But I needed to respond in some way, so I decided to do two things: 1) Write this book, and 2) Vow to do my very best never to be the kind of leader described in that letter.

I'm happy (even jolly) to say I've done both. Writing this book was by far the easier of the two responses; living up to my vow—turning my good intentions into predictable behaviors—was more challenging. It took abandoning a few old behaviors and adopting a few new ones; it required commitment, self-discipline, concentration, and prioritization. And I needed to monitor my progress (and still do), through both self-evaluation and periodic feedback from the workshop team, by providing answers to the following:

In the last several months, what have I done to...

* Be accessible (physically and mentally) to employees who would like my attention?
* Be considerate of staff-member needs?
* Provide employees with the training, tools, resources, and feedback required for success?
* Keep employees in the "what's happening" information loop?
* Help team members maintain an appropriate

balance between their professional and
personal lives?

❋ Demonstrate respect for employees' time and
talents…as well as respect for them
as individuals?

❋ Solicit, and listen to, staff-member ideas
and concerns?

❋ Help everyone develop and grow?

❋ Fairly distribute the work and workload?

These, and many others like them, are the questions I ask—and the things I do—to make sure I focus on the wonderful workers who comprise our wonderful workshop. What questions do *you* ask? What action items would I find on *your* list?

Let Values Be Your Guide

Every once in a while, a truly special moment occurs in education—the *student* turns out to be the *teacher*. I experienced one of those moments not too long ago, and I'd like to share it with you. This next leadership lesson comes courtesy of a savvy little elf named Virginia.

Build a Wonderful Workshop

It was a Tuesday morning and I was conducting a leadership development training session in the workshop classroom. I gave each participant a set of plastic building blocks along with an assignment: "Build a model of a wonderful workshop." The purpose of the task was twofold:

1. Test student creativity and thinking, and
2. Provide me with ideas for improving our North Pole facility.

After starting the exercise, I left the room.

I returned an hour later and found that everyone was busy building his or her structure—everyone, that is, except Virginia. She was just sitting there, staring into space. "Is there a problem, Virginia?" I inquired. "No, Santa," she replied, "I'm just thinking." So I left her to her thoughts and exited the classroom.

After another hour had passed, I returned to the room to conclude the exercise. As I moved from table to table, I was truly impressed by the array of detailed models with structural components like smokestacks, loading ramps, conveyor belts, sleigh landing pads, cafeterias, gyms, offices, and even high-tech classrooms.

When I came to Virginia's model, however, I was taken aback. There, in front of her, were six vertical columns—and nothing more. "Need more time?" I asked. "No thanks," she answered, "I'm done." Hearing that, I probed further: "Virginia, I'm not sure I understand. All the other models are very detailed structures, but all you have are six columns. No walls, no roof, no nothing. How come?" The explanation she offered is where you'll find the lesson for leaders everywhere:

"Well, Santa, it seems to me that what makes a workshop wonderful is not walls and ceilings, but what happens *inside* those walls and *under* those ceilings…it's not how a workshop *stands*, but what it *stands for* that makes it special. These six columns you see are pillars, and they represent values—the values of respect, integrity, quality, customer service, responsibility, and teamwork. I found them listed on our website. Maybe for some folks they're just words, but for me, they're blueprints to follow. And that's where leadership comes in. **Making sure that**

everyone knows what values are important, and then **helping everyone turn those good beliefs into everyday behaviors** is how leaders create a great place to work. At least that's how I see it. And that's why my model looks the way it does. Did I do okay?"

With a huge grin on my face and a twinkle in my eye, I responded: "Yes, Virginia, that *is* a wonderful workshop. And I think that you are going to be a wonderful leader. Thank you for giving me such a valuable gift."

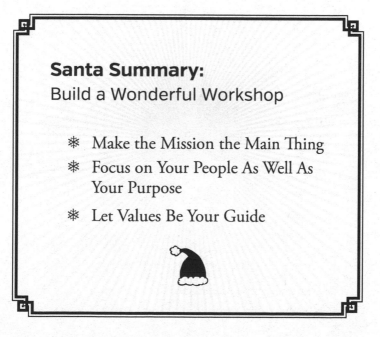

Santa Summary:
Build a Wonderful Workshop

❆ Make the Mission the Main Thing
❆ Focus on Your People As Well As Your Purpose
❆ Let Values Be Your Guide

CHOOSE YOUR REINDEER WISELY

Hire Tough So You Can Manage Easy

You know Dasher and Dancer, Prancer and Vixen; Comet and Cupid, Donner and Blitzen. But do you recall the *least* famous reindeer of all: Misfit? Probably not. He's not here anymore. Unfortunately, I had to let him go decades ago. But I certainly learned a lot from the whole Misfit experience.

It all started when I was faced with hiring a new reindeer to fill a vacant position. Now, I know that pulling the sleigh is a very important job. Ask the reindeer—they'll tell you. But I was busy—very busy. Recruiting and hiring a new puller was just one of the scores of things on Santa's platter. And besides, bringing on new staff can be tedious, bureaucratic, and tiring work. It's not what makes me jolly. Personally, I'd much rather walk around the workshop, chat with the elves, and test the new toys. So, I took the easy route. I did a cursory résumé review, conducted a quick, pro forma interview, and grabbed the first warm, antlered-body that appeared halfway decent.

Did I probe to determine if Misfit was committed to responsibilities like teamwork, dependability, and customer service? No. Did I test his flying skills? No. Did I do a thorough background check? No. Did I involve any of the other reindeer in the selection process? No. Did I take one of our new, high-pressure water gun toys and shoot myself in the proverbial foot? *YES!*

Misfit was appropriately named all right. After a short period of putting his best hoof forward, the problems began. He'd show up late, and then display a less than desirable attitude when I called him on it. More and more, he'd carry less and less of his share of the load. That made the sleigh pull to the right—forcing the left side crew to work harder in order for us to stay straight. The harder they worked, the more irritated they became…and the harder it was for me to keep the reins in check.

Choose Your Reindeer Wisely

I ended up spending way too much time watching Misfit, re-re-re-training him, counseling him, and handling complaints about him from the other reindeer—and the elves as well. Pretty soon, he was bringing the whole team down. And productivity was going down with them. All of that because of one Misfit reindeer…all of that because I cut corners and allowed joining the team to be way too easy.

That was then. Now I do things much differently. Through the Misfit experience, I've come to realize that:

1. Because it's employees who ultimately make our mission happen, staffing is my single most important responsibility.
2. The time I spend hiring the right way is nothing compared to the time I'll *have* to spend dealing with the wrong reindeer.

Take a hiring lesson from Santa. Invest in doing it right up front and everyone—especially you—will be happier down the road.

Promote the Right Ones...for the Right Reasons

Just listen to his cute little song (go ahead...sing it to yourself) and you'll quickly realize that Rudolph wasn't always the lead reindeer. In fact, he didn't get that promotion until one foggy night about a century ago. Before that, Donner had the top spot; Donner was "the deer." And as it turned out, promoting Donner was "the problem."

Now don't get me wrong, Donner was not a bad reindeer. He was a great reindeer! One of the best pullers I've ever had. He was strong, fast, and dependable; he pulled more than his weight (and he weighed a ton). He followed instructions to the letter. Donner was a pro—as a puller. So when it came time to promote a new lead, he was my obvious choice. He had earned it. And I assumed that the best puller would make the best leader. Well, to quote another old song title, "it ain't necessarily so." And he proved it.

To say that Donner had a difficult time is an understatement. The lead job was different than the puller job—with skill and ability requirements that I hadn't tested for and that he couldn't meet.

Choose Your Reindeer Wisely

He was in over his head, and he was miserable. So were the other reindeer...and so was I. It's no secret that I was a little short on the "Ho, Ho, Ho's" during that period. Donner needed to go back to the job he was good at, and a new lead—the right lead—needed to be found.

Lead reindeer ("RD1"on our classification sheet) is an important position. The lead has more contact with the pullers than anyone else here at the Pole... and a lot more influence over them as well. It was critical that I pick a leader that the other deer would follow. And there stood Rudolph.

Rudolph was a decent puller, but by no means was he the strongest or fastest of the crew. When he first joined the team, some of the other reindeer laughed, called him names, and excluded him from their games. They're not an easy bunch to "bond" with. But that changed as they (and I) began to notice that there was something special about Rudolph; he seemed to have a knack for getting things done with others...a nose for leadership. So I decided to consider him for the lead.

This time, I started to take some notes. I created two columns: 1) The tasks, duties, and responsibilities of the lead position, and 2) The characteristics, talents, values, abilities, and attitudes that I felt were necessary to perform those tasks successfully—and to support our overall mission. Then I tested Rudolph and the other candidates against those criteria. He was a standout. He had "the right stuff."

So, on that foggy night long ago, Rudolph got his shot. And the rest, as they say, is history. It's a *wonderful* history…and an unforgettable lesson.

Go for the Diversity Advantage

Not all of what I've learned about hiring came from reindeer experiences. And since our other group of workers tend to get a little miffed if they don't get equal time, here's Santa's third and final lesson on employee selection—involving the elves:

It used to be that our elves were pretty much all alike—same size, same pointed ears, same little green suits, same way of talking…same everything. Whenever we needed new elves, I automatically looked for, and brought on, workers that fit the standard mold. Why not? That's the way it was for years and years—and it seemed to be working just fine. We rarely messed up an order and we had never missed our December 24 delivery. I was one happy sleigh driver—that is, until two things happened.

First, I found out that we had competitors. Department stores, online retailers, discount chains, and a whole host of other manufacturers and toy distributors were moving in on the market we had cornered for decades. They had all kinds of workers (not just elves), and they were gaining ground on our operation. To add insult to injury, some of them were actually using phony Santas—imposters dressed up like me...pretending to be me.

I wasn't sure how to address the challenge of competition, but I knew that *something* needed to be done. Staying with "business as usual" probably wouldn't serve us well that much longer.

Soon after discovering that we had competition, the second thing happened: a group of North Pole politicians (yes, we have them too) passed a law that said we had to expand our hiring practices; we had to start bringing on "different" kinds of toy makers—not just the little pointy-eared fellas we'd been employing forever.

So we complied with the regulations and came face-to-face with a *new* set of challenges. We had *not-the-same-old-elves* recruiting procedures to develop and coworker acceptance issues to deal with. Since not everyone spoke Northpolese, there were some language barriers. New interpersonal skills had to be developed. And things called "nondiscrimination regulations" had to be communicated, taught, and followed.

It wasn't easy, but we did it. We did it all. And in the process, we got more than a Santa's sackful of unexpected benefits. It didn't take long to discover that our "different" toy makers came bearing gifts. They brought new skills, perspectives, and ideas to the workshop. They gave us more than one way of thinking, planning, producing, and problem solving. They made us better, stronger, and much more in touch with the "different" shapes, sizes, and colors of customers that we serve. And all that has helped us more than hold our own with all those competing Santa wannabes out there.

What started out as a challenging situation—to merely comply with a requirement—has become our most significant competitive advantage. And it can be yours as well. Believe Santa Claus…believe in diversity.

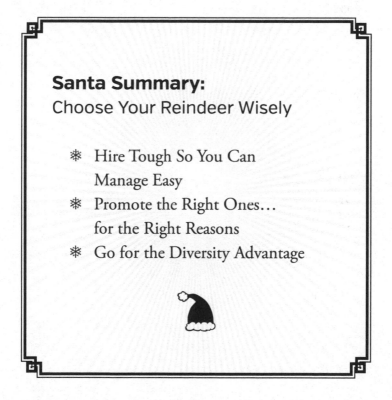

Santa Summary:
Choose Your Reindeer Wisely

❄ Hire Tough So You Can Manage Easy
❄ Promote the Right Ones… for the Right Reasons
❄ Go for the Diversity Advantage

MAKE A LIST AND CHECK IT TWICE

Plan Your Work

Respond to endless streams of request letters, make millions of high-quality products—according to exact specifications—364 days a year, package the toys so they arrive in perfect condition, and deliver the exact right gift to the exact right person in the exact right house millions of times in one single night. Then, immediately begin working on the next season's demands—which inevitably include *more* kids, *more* homes, an *expanded* service area, and *fewer* (and smaller) chimneys. That's what we do every year. We do it flawlessly…and none of it happens by accident. Our success—and resulting reputation for excellence—is the result of clearly defined goals combined with well-thought out plans to accomplish those goals.

We begin by breaking down our one huge annual goal (our mission) of "delivering the goods" into a series of manageable, bite-size subgoals. We have them for the shop in general, the teams within the shop, and individuals within the teams.

Whether in direct production and delivery, or a "behind the scenes" support function, *everyone* has goals—including me. Our goals are specific yet flexible—allowing for changing conditions and circumstances. And because staff "buy-in" and commitment are so important to achieving our objectives, I make sure that *everyone* has input in the goal-setting process.

Once our individual and group goals are identified, we move into the planning (making "the list") phase. Plans provide us with the direction, focus, and organization we need to stay on task. And since none of us here at the Pole have perfect memories, we make sure they're *written* action plans.

We develop our plans by answering six questions for each set goal:

1. **What** needs to be accomplished?
2. **Why** does it need to be done? (How does it contribute to our overall mission?)

3. **When** does it need to be accomplished?
4. **Where** am I/are we now in relation to this goal?
5. **Who** will be involved in accomplishing this?
6. **How** will it be accomplished? (What specific steps and activities are involved, and what resources are required?)

After answering these questions with as much detail as possible, we perform the last of the planning activities: adding contingencies. We do our best to anticipate the unexpected by asking *But what if...* questions. *But what if the snowfall is way above or below normal this year? But what if a flu bug works its way through the shop during peak production time? But what if the computer with our delivery address book crashes?* Certainly we can't predict all the obstacles we may face, but combining some thought with past experiences does enhance our readiness to deal with that fellow Murphy's Law.

Work Your Plan

Several years ago, in an effort to meet our growing production demands, we started making "assembly required" toys. We spent a great deal of time and effort developing detailed instruction booklets that even a child could follow. But then, we started to receive lots and lots of emails, with attached photos (of final products that looked nothing like our original designs), claiming that our toys were faulty. We investigated. The problem was that the *children* weren't doing the assembly—the *parents* were. And they were ignoring the instructions. The plans we had worked so hard to create were, in many cases, useless. They had become nothing more than an academic exercise because they weren't being followed. The key learning: ya gotta follow the plans—whether you're assembling toys or working to achieve your goals. We most definitely have put that learning to good use. So should you.

Once a reasonable plan is made, we immediately implement it. Acting quickly is an imperative for our business. Don't get me wrong, we *do* think things through carefully. But we're also careful to avoid the "paralysis of analysis" that often accompanies the pursuit of elusive plan perfection. We get things going fast, and then we make midcourse corrections as necessary. And the way we know how we're doing, as well as what adjustments we need to make, is through continual monitoring and measurement.

None of us here at the workshop are particularly fond of negative surprises—especially me. They take the twinkle right out of my eyes. Fact is, we face enough challenges already without manufacturing any more on our own. So we don't wait until estimated completion dates to see if we've reached our goals. Once we make our list (plan), we check it twice. Actually, we check it a lot *more* than twice.

We schedule (as in, set specific times on our calendars) frequent progress checks as part of the work-planning process. I meet with teams and individuals—and they meet among themselves, without me—to measure the status of our goals against predetermined progress "benchmarks." At those meetings, we ask the following:

* Is each goal still valid and doable?
* Are we where we should be in terms of attaining each goal?

❄ Have any conditions or circumstances
   changed since we originally set each goal?
❄ Do we need to make any changes to our goals,
   our action plans, or our performance levels?

The answers to these questions provide the intelligence we need to guide us in bringing our important mission to life.

As the sign on our workshop wall says:

If We Want to Hear Jingle Bells Ringing on the 24th, We Need to Set and Live by Goals...All Year Long!

Make the Most of What You Have

There's another sign hanging in our workshop. It reads:

So Many Toys, So Little Time

It serves as a reminder for us (and a clue for you) about overcoming big challenges and accomplishing big goals: you have to maximize the resources available to you.

Make a List and Check It Twice

Goal setting—planning your work and then working your plan—not only leads to effectiveness, it also fosters efficiency…it helps you minimize waste. And if there's one thing we hate around here, it's waste. Considering the volume of orders and deliveries we deal with annually, we'd quickly go out of business if we didn't make the absolute best use of our resources: time, money, materials, and the talents of our elves and reindeer. I can picture the headlines now: *SANTA WASTES AWAY TO NOTHING!* (And they would not be talking about my belly that shakes like a bowl full of jelly!)

Because resources are so important to us, we've gone well beyond merely relying on goal action plans to ensure efficiency. The best example of this is a workshop-wide team we created called "Waste Watchers" (again, no connection with my girth). The sole purpose of the group is to identify and eliminate inefficient/wasteful business practices. The following presents just a few of the strategies they've come up with to help us do more with less. I offer it as yet another gift to you.

Making the Most of *TIME*

➻ Prioritize tasks (do the most important things first) and use "to do" lists to organize daily activities.

➻ Start and end meetings promptly—and issue agendas in advance.

➻ Teach time-management skills and techniques. Take advantage of timesaving technology.

Making the Most of *MONEY*

➻ Buy in discounted bulk whenever appropriate.

➻ Shop for the best prices on materials, supplies, equipment, and services.

➻ Communicate electronically to reduce long-distance charges.

➻ Think pennies as well as dollars—a few cents saved here and there add up quickly.

Making the Most of *MATERIALS* and *EQUIPMENT*

➻ "Measure twice, cut once."

➻ Reuse and recycle whenever possible.

➻ Be religious about preventative maintenance.

➻ Invest in extended warranties.

Making the Most of *EMPLOYEE TALENT* and *EXPERTISE*

➡ Involve the *people* with the *knowledge* in the *decisions*.

➡ Match jobs with worker skills and interests.

➡ Enhance employee expertise through training and developmental assignments.

➡ Encourage employees to share their knowledge with others.

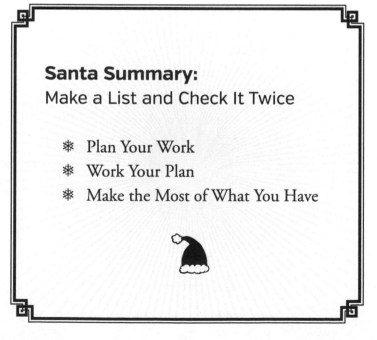

Santa Summary:
Make a List and Check It Twice

❄ Plan Your Work
❄ Work Your Plan
❄ Make the Most of What You Have

LISTEN TO THE ELVES

Open Your Ears to Participation

Way, way back when we started in this business, there were a lot less orders to fill and a lot fewer houses to visit. We didn't have even 10 percent of the staff we have now, and I did quite a bit of the toy making myself. In fact, I did quite a bit of *everything* myself. But eventually, as our operation grew in size and complexity, it became necessary to move away from "doing" (except for my big deliveries) and devote my time to managing. The good news was that I had a wealth of experience to call upon as a manager. The bad news: I used that experience…to a fault.

Because I had "been there," I was pretty sure I knew more than—or at least as much as—the elves did about toy production. Don't get me wrong—I was always kind and respectful to my employees. I was quite fond of those little folks in green. Still am. But when a decision needed to be made, it was me alone who made it; when a process needed to be modified or upgraded, I devised the plan; when a color needed to be added, I determined the paint mixture; when new equipment needed to be selected...oh well, you get the picture. Running the show was my job. Besides, who else could make those calls? Certainly not the elves. They had neither the experience for, nor the interest in, administrative work like that. Or so I thought. Until, that is, one day when out in the workshop there arose such a clatter, I sprang from my office to see what was the matter.

It turns out, the gears of the toy production line had grinded to an unexpected halt. The inspection process that *I* had just implemented (after two weeks of closed-door design) was slowing things to a snail's pace. The elves were going crazy trying to keep up with the production schedule. And then, the new mechanical assembler that *I* researched and purchased let loose with a strange thumping noise, coughed up a billow of smoke, and shut down completely.

A quick investigation revealed that my new procedure and the assembly machine were both flawed.

"We could have told you," said one of the elves, "if you just had asked us in the beginning…and really listened to what we had to say." I responded: "So what can we do to get things going again?" With that, a bunch of them huddled for a little while and came up with a better inspection process—and some modifications that got the assembler up and running again. We were back in business; the elves were patting each other on the back and smiling. And I had come to realize that involving workers in running the operation—and in making decisions that affect them—is a key strategy for leadership success.

Now I ask for (and listen to) the elves' ideas and opinions on most everything we do. I even let *them* make many of the toy-making decisions we face. And the production line has never run better.

Pay Attention to How You're Perceived

I want this…I want that; Last year's gift was great. This year I'd really like…; Dear Santa, you are a very nice person. Please bring me…

That's just a small sampling of the kind of customer feedback I'm constantly receiving here at the North Pole. Do I pay attention to it? You bet your boots (or my boots) I do! It's part of what keeps us in business. Couldn't operate without it. Knowing what people want and need—and especially what they think of us—is critical to our success. And, as mentioned in the previous pages, I've come to realize the importance of listening not only to our customers, but also to our elves, reindeer, and others in Santa's workshop.

As our challenges have grown with each new season, more and more I rely on teamwork, collaboration, and the contributions of each member of the workshop team. Ensuring that those things happen requires effective leadership on my part, and I began to wonder how I was doing on that front. The only way to find out was to ask…and then listen.

So, I began doing employee attitude surveys and conducting focus groups. I even established a "North Pole feedback hotline" to help find out what everyone thought about me as a leader, and to provide a vehicle for collecting input on how I could improve.

Listen to the Elves

When designing the survey, I went to the professors at NPU (North Pole University) for assistance with question development. I even hired a consultant group to help me organize and interpret the information.

Input forwarded via the hotline pinpointed two key requirements necessary for making the process work: 1) I had to constructively accept the feedback I received, and 2) I needed to *ACT* on the information—to use it as a catalyst for becoming a more effective leader, and for developing a better organization.

Neither of those requirements was particularly easy at first. But it was clear that failing to meet them would hamper my staff's willingness to candidly share their feelings and would turn the effort into a meaningless exercise. That would be worse than doing nothing at all.

So I listened...and I acted. I do to this very day. And I'm a much better Santa because of it. I pay attention to what my elves (and others) feel. Perceptions are realities for those that hold them... and I must deal with those realities in order to lead effectively. And so, too, must you.

Whether it's through formal surveys, hotlines, informal discussions, "slip me an anonymous note about my leadership" invitations, or whatever, you must find your own way to ask, listen, and act.

Walk Awhile in *Their* Shoes

It's true that I'm in the gift-giving business. That's what I do…it's what I live for. But occasionally, I *get* gifts as well. And like everyone else, Santa does have his favorites. My most cherished gift of all occupies a place of prominence on a bookshelf in my office: a pair of green felt elf shoes (the kind with pointed toes that curl up). I received them several years ago. They just appeared on my desk one day, along with a "Dear Santa" letter.

Now this letter was much different than the kind I'm used to reading. It didn't ask for anything. It was a thank-you letter. I consider it a written commendation. And with great pride, I offer it as your next leadership lesson:

Dear Santa,

Thank you for being such a great boss. We know it isn't easy being you—with all the pressures and responsibilities that you have. We also know that we're not always the easiest bunch to deal with. But with all that you have going on, and with all that we sometimes throw your way, you still manage to remain considerate and understanding. You show us, by your behaviors, that you realize it's challenging for all of us in the workshop too. That makes us appreciate you even more.

We really do look forward to your regular visits to the shop floor. We like it when you stop to chat with each of us to see how things are going. It hasn't always been that way, but that doesn't matter. It's that way now, and we're grateful that it is.

It's great when you ask us about the problems, challenges, and obstacles that we face in filling our orders and meeting deadlines. You really listen—showing us that our feelings are important...that we are important.

We like it when you occasionally work next to us—giving us a hand and keeping you in touch with the operation. But the thing we appreciate most is when you ask what you can do to make things easier and better for us, and better for the workshop—and then you do those that are reasonable and appropriate.

Thank you, Santa, for making the effort to see things through our eyes...for walking in these smaller, yet none-the-less import-ant shoes. Your feet may not fit in them, but your heart most definitely does.

The Elves

Santa Summary:
Listen to the Elves

* Open Your Ears to Participation
* Pay Attention to How You're Perceived
* Walk Awhile in *Their* Shoes

SAY HO HO HO, BUT DON'T FORGET THE SNOW

Build Contagious Enthusiasm

I discovered years ago that a workshop filled with Ho Ho Ho's is not only a more enjoyable place to work but also one that is more positive and productive. Elves and reindeer working together with smiles on their faces are contagious. But that outcome doesn't happen by accident or some type of magic. Making it a reality begins with me, *Santa the Chief Cheerleader*!

A key part of my leadership responsibility is regularly dedicating time to give recognition…to catching our team members doing things right—and letting them know they've been "caught" performing well. It's amazing how the simple act of recognizing and thanking employees puts an even broader smile on their faces—and mine as well.

But there's another reality that comes into play here: I am only one red-suited jolly old guy here at the North Pole. And, as with so many other aspects of our business, I can only do so much by myself. So to truly build a workshop that is filled with positive energy, I not only need to set the example individually, but also make the goal of recognizing positive performance part of *EVERY* reindeer and elf's job expectations. And that's just what I've done—along with establishing a set of guidelines ("Santa's Recognition Rules") for everyone to follow in order to provide effective, high-quality recognition.

And the more I show them how to do that and "recognize the recognizers" myself, the more promoting contagious enthusiasm becomes just a regular part of everyone's job.

Santa's Recognition Rules

MAKE IT *Timely*
Give recognition as soon as possible. Don't wait until later because sometimes "later" never comes.

GET *Specific*
Tell recognition recipients exactly what they did that was positive. A mere "Good job, Rudolph" really doesn't say that much.

BE *Appreciative*
Tell team members what their positive performance means to you, to the other elves and reindeer, and to the goals of the workshop—and thank them for that.

GET *Personal*
Adjust the style and method of your recognition to the receiver. Give "different strokes to different folks."

MAKE IT *Proportional*
Match the type and amount of recognition with the value and impact of the achievement.

Expect the Unexpected

All the positive workplace energy you can create cannot help you totally avoid the inevitable obstacles to workshop success. For example, three years ago on our delivery day, two reindeer came down with "Flyers Flu." Oops…what do we do? Well, we *HAD* to find a solution and we did. Then there was the time we lost power in the workshop, the first week of December, when the entire line of toys was being finished. We *HAD* to find a solution and we did!

Our biggest unexpected event, however, happened just last year.

At the North Pole, we have snow. *LOTS* of snow! But last year, we had a *MEGA* snowfall—one some called "a thousand year blizzard." So the morning before the Big Delivery we got the workshop and sleigh teams together to talk about this challenge and how we might solve the problem.

The first hoof raised and voice we heard came from "Donner the Downer," claiming that the snow was way too high and that this obstacle was unsolvable. He then suggested that we needed to move our delivery date to sometime in January. Hmmm. I bit my tongue and waited a moment. And I'm glad I did. Suddenly, dozens of waving hands and hooves were raised as team members began to try to out-shout each other. One of those hands belonged to Little Larry from the Stuffed Toy Section.

After being called on and given the floor, Larry talked about all the people who were counting on our on-time delivery—and how "Delaying our deliveries is just not an option." And then, pointing to a series of signs we had posted around the workshop, he asked: "Don't you remember these?"

It's the Things That You Least Expect That Hit You the Hardest

---

Life's Not Always Fair, So Build a Bridge and Get over It!

If It Was Easy, Anyone Could Do It!

Problems Are Opportunities in Disguise!

There Are Always Solutions!

Do It Now Because Sometimes "Later" Can Easily Become "Never." Complaining Doesn't Solve Problems, Doing Does!

Get Problems Solved...Together

Because we had such a positive "make it happen" workplace culture, everyone (except Donner at the beginning) wanted to view this unexpected event as a challenge that we—with some creative thinking—could solve together.

We all knew the importance of our delivery date, and that if it was changed, children around the world would be incredibly disappointed. So clearly we *HAD* to find a solution. As all this was playing out, I was watching Donner's expression change from sad to supportive. In fact, he was the first one to begin offering possible solutions to our unexpected dilemma. Other team members began to chime in. One idea led to another...and another. Bewilderment had quickly become excitement. And a music-to-my-ears chant started and increased in intensity: "We can do this. We can do this. *WE* can do this!"

Contagious enthusiasm was rearing its *beautiful* head!

As a result of our challenge, a team of warehouse elves suggested, and then rigged up, a supersized snow plough to clear the landing strip behind the shop. The back-up reindeer volunteered to make up a sleigh team of sixteen for the stormy evening take-off. We added an aerodynamic "roof rack" device to the back of the sleigh so we could double our cargo load of presents. Rudolph—working with Gilda, our IT elf—installed the latest GPS system to help guide the team through the treacherous storm. And Mrs. Claus came up with a container which doubled the amount of hot chocolate we could take with us to keep us warm throughout the night. *WOW*!

The beauty of this experience was that while it all was all happening, I was saying *NOTHING*. I didn't have to because everyone understood the severity of the dilemma, the importance of our mission, and the necessity of being fully committed to finding solutions—together! I just helped everyone get whatever they needed, offered advice and suggestions when asked, got out of the way, and assumed that all important role of *Santa the Cheerleader*.

Needless to say (but I'll say it anyway), I was very proud because we were getting good stuff done and the workshop team was taking the lead.

My learning here is that Ho Ho Ho's are great for immediate effects, but even more importantly, they're vital for establishing a workshop culture that is built on pride, professionalism, and individual commitment.

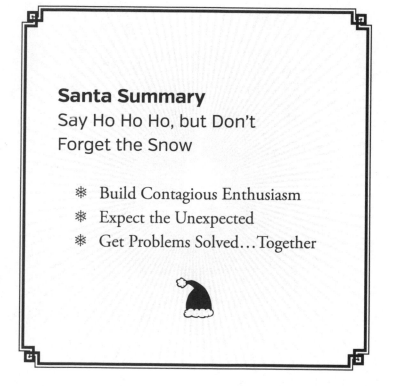

Santa Summary
Say Ho Ho Ho, but Don't
Forget the Snow

* Build Contagious Enthusiasm
* Expect the Unexpected
* Get Problems Solved…Together

GIVE THEM GIFTS THAT LAST A LIFETIME

Teach Success Skills

It was several years ago, but I remember it like it was just yesterday. That's when I learned an invaluable lesson in leadership from Ian—a candidate who would end up being selected as my EICOT ("Elf In Charge Of Training").

During the interview, Ian reversed roles and asked *me* a question. "Santa, what do you see as the purpose of training here at the workshop?" "That's easy," I replied, "It's to teach all of our team members how to do their jobs." I could tell by the look on his face that Ian had some concern about my answer. "Don't you agree?" I asked. That's when Ian provided me with the lesson I have never forgotten—one that got him the job…one that I pass along to you.

"Well Santa, the way I see it," answered Ian, "developing our team is about more than just teaching folks how to do their jobs; it's also about teaching them how to be *successful*. And there is a difference between those two concepts." Now my interest was piqued. "Tell me more," I probed.

"To be sure," Ian replied, "we have to make sure that team members have the knowledge and skills necessary to do their jobs well. Elves must know things like how to make toys and load the sleigh properly. Reindeer must be skilled at pulling that sleigh through take-offs, landings, and long night flights. And then there's the others—the bookkeepers, the sleigh mechanics, the kitchen staff, the laundry department, etc., etc., etc. Everyone here at the Pole has a job to do and we all must know how to perform our assigned functions with the highest level of quality. But..." (I knew there was a "but" coming) "...it seems to me that in order to be truly successful, we all need more than just the technical skills of our job classifications."

Give Them Gifts That Last a Lifetime

To clarify his point, Ian asked me a series of questions:

Is an elf really successful if he or she makes good toys but doesn't get along well with others and communicates poorly?

Is a reindeer really successful if he or she pulls hard but isn't a team player who helps others succeed?

Are any of us truly successful if we're good at our crafts but display negative attitudes or fail to solve problems effectively?

I didn't have to think long or hard to answer those queries: "No," "No," and "*NO!*" Point made... point clear.

As a result of that one meeting, Ian got the training job...and I got a valuable lesson. As leaders, we must identify *ALL* of the factors and characteristics that comprise employee success—and help team members learn, grow, and develop the skills we want them to have in each of those areas.

Under Ian's direction, we have widened the scope of our orientation agenda to include training and developmental activities in "beyond our crafts" arenas. And the positive results speak for themselves.

As the sign on Ian's office wall says:

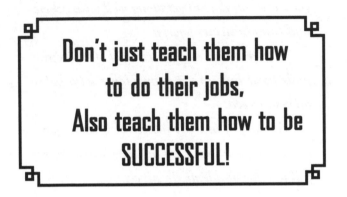

Don't just teach them how
to do their jobs.
Also teach them how to be
SUCCESSFUL!

Reinforce Relationships

'Twas a month before our big night, when all through the North Pole I assumed elves were busy—every last single soul. I reviewed children's letters—a whole pile on my lap. And then I was ready for a well-deserved nap. When out in the shop there arose such a clatter, I sprang from my chair to see what was the matter. And what to my wondering eyes should appear: two elves going at it with some upset reindeer!

THIS WAS NOT GOOD! Not only had the "combatants" stopped working, but their friction had a negative spill-over effect on the other workers—causing production to slow to a snail's pace.

Now I have always stressed that good interpersonal relationships are critical to maintaining both a positive working environment and high-quality performance. But I've also learned, through experience, that:

1. Occasional squabbles between workers are inevitable.
2. Most workers need help resolving those squabbles.
3. It's my job, as their leader, to help them repair what's broken.

So I called the involved parties up to my office for one of my "Santa intervention" chats. The first thing I did was to share my observations of what had happened—emphasizing how their coworkers and productivity were negatively impacted. After explaining the problem, I told them how valuable they were to me—and how important it was that they work well together in order for us to accomplish our truly important mission. Next, I clarified that it was *their* responsibility to resolve *their* conflict. Finally, I introduced them to—and helped them work through—my **CALM** Model for conflict resolution.

Santa's CALM Model

Clarify the Issue
(Think it through yourself)

> What am I upset about? What actually happened?

> What am I feeling? Why do I feel that way?

> How might I have contributed to the problem?

> What are my long-term desired outcomes for the situation?

Address the Problem
(Share your feelings with the other person)

> Here's what happened...

> Here's how that made me feel...

> Here's how it negatively impacted me, my work, and others...

Listen to the Other Side
[Understand his/her feelings]

> Give your total attention. Never interrupt.

> Ask questions [for clarification only].

> Focus on understanding rather than convincing.

Manage Your Way to Resolution
[Decide what you'll do]

> Agree that a problem exists.

> Identify each other's concerns and needs.

> Explore possible win-win solutions.

> Focus on what's right, **not** who's right.

> Agree on a course of action.

> Determine how missteps will be handled.

> Close on a positive note.

Push Pride and Professionalism

It's no secret that all of us here at the North Pole are in the gift business. We make gifts (mostly toys), we stock gifts, and we deliver gifts on that very special night each year. Most of the presents we provide have a limited shelf (i.e., interest) life and are "outgrown" within a year or two. Occasionally, however, the gifts we bring are kept and cherished forever—like dolls that are collected and passed down through generations. Those are "lifetime gifts"—the most precious things we create. And, as an analogy, they provide a vitally important lesson for all of us who share the treasured title *LEADER*.

As leaders, everything we do affects and impacts those whom we lead. When we do our jobs well— with our team members' best interests paramount in our minds—we're actually providing our people with gifts: the gifts of great leadership. And when our activities are geared toward helping our employees learn, grow, and develop the work habits of success, we're giving those who rely on us gifts which will serve them well throughout their careers…gifts that last a lifetime.

Based on the feedback I have received from my reindeer and elves—including those who have left us to accept advancement positions with other major toy producers—one of the most appreciated lifetime gifts I have given my staff is a continual emphasis on *PRIDE* and *PROFESSIONALISM*. We teach those concepts, we discuss them, we expect them, we reward them, and we quickly address the infrequent times when they are found to be lacking within our operation. All of that emphasis and attention begins for each team member on their very first day when, at new-hire orientation, I share the following thoughts and beliefs…

"Everything you do here at our workshop bears your personal signature. Each action you take—the way you complete every task, assignment, project, or job duty—is a reflection of *YOU*. And that fact leads to two questions everyone needs to ponder and be concerned with:

1. What does my 'personal signature' look like?
2. Does it portray someone who exhibits pride in him/herself and the work they perform?

"Take a moment and think about individuals you feel are or have been truly successful at work. Pick a couple of them…picture them in your minds.

Now, answer those same two questions as they apply to your success role models.

"Are these people who cut corners, just do the bare minimum to get by, and aren't concerned about quality? Of course not! They are team members who *CARE.* They care about their coworkers; they care about their customers; they care about their jobs and organizations. Most importantly, they care about *THEMSELVES!* They understand that respect is not something just to be given to others. We must have it for ourselves as well.

"Take a blank sheet of paper and write your signature on it.

"Now look at it...stare at it...think about it. What does that signature stand for? What kind of work does it represent? What professional reputation comes with it? Make it meaningful—because it *is* attached to everything you do."

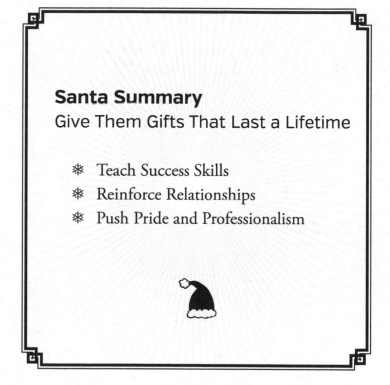

Santa Summary
Give Them Gifts That Last a Lifetime

* ❄ Teach Success Skills
* ❄ Reinforce Relationships
* ❄ Push Pride and Professionalism

GET BEYOND THE RED WAGONS

Help Everyone Accept the Reality of Change

There's an old saying (although it wasn't old when I first heard it…and neither was I) that goes like this: the only constant in life and in business is *CHANGE*. And for those of us who live and work at the North Pole, nothing exemplifies that saying more than "red wagons."

It used to be that one of the most popular toys we produced and delivered (thirty-seven percent of our production activities to be exact) was shiny red wagons. Just about every child dreamed of getting one for the holidays. Maybe *you* had one when you were little. If so, there's a good chance it came from us. The elves made tons of them. They loved to make them…they were good at making them… they took pride in watching them roll off the assembly line. They were a happy little bunch of "wagon masters"—until the day I had to tell them that, based on the letters I was receiving, the demand for wagons was way down. Video games were "in," and the workshop crew needed to change what they did and how they operated.

I wasn't looking forward to being the messenger on that one. It was going to be a major shake-up that would force the elves out of their comfort zones and throw them into the new and unknown. I knew we had to abandon the status quo. And as the leader, I had to make it happen with both decisiveness and sensitivity. To keep the same level of commitment they had shown to red wagons, I couldn't just dictate change, I had to orchestrate it. That involved applying several strategies—ones I've replicated many times in response to the never-ending need to move in new directions.

First, I complimented the elves on their history of red wagon excellence and expressed my pride in their past accomplishments. *Next,* I introduced the change we were facing and explained *why* it was necessary. I laid out the facts—the raw data and evidence—and asked if anyone interpreted the information differently than I did. After some discussion, they acknowledged (some begrudgingly) that my read was correct. *Then*, we discussed the benefits to be gained—individually and collectively—for making the required change. Of course, the two biggest benefits were "staying in business" and "staying employed." Immediately *after that*, I asked for everyone's commitment to the new direction...and got it. I reciprocated with two commitments of my own: 1) To provide the training and support that employees would need to make the changes—and feel good about themselves in the process, and 2) To demonstrate patience and understanding as they worked their way through the new learning curve. *Finally*, I made sure that everyone on the team understood that change of this nature was inevitable—we had no choice whether or not it would come. Our only choice was how we responded to it.

How have they responded? Just see what's out there next holiday season. You'll find a lot more than red wagons...and an equal amount of smiling little faces!

Remember: The Customer Is Really in Charge

There are many catalysts for the changes we continually have to make. Some come from the development of new technology and equipment that allow us to do our jobs better and faster—like our board game shrink wrapper and labeler. Others come from the analysis of ideas and strategies that didn't work—like our toy Pinto campaign. (We found thousands of them under trees one year later with notes saying: "You can have this back.") Several of our changes are spurred by monitoring the successes and failures of our competition. And still others are the result of hiring new employees who bring new ideas and experiences with them to the workshop. But unquestionably, the largest number of the changes we face and make originate from the need to respond to our customers—as with the red wagon situation.

Like you, we are—first and foremost—in the customer service business. For us, no customers equals no business. If the people we serve were to stop writing, close their fireplace dampers, and disappear from the sleigh's radar screen, we would eventually vanish as well. Obviously, our job is to give people what they're looking for. And as their wants and needs change, we have to change along with them. Doing that starts with accepting the fact that the customer is truly in charge of our business, and then continues by setting into place plans for looking outside our snow-covered walls to make sure we have our fingers on the pulse of the market.

For us, the name of the game quickly became *field trips*…a lot more field trips than the once-a-year pilgrimage experienced only by me, a harness full of reindeer, and the couple of elves who ride shotgun on the sleigh.

We do *virtual* field trips—through letters, emails, telephone calls, and internet research. And we do *actual* field trips where, on a rotational basis, we send employees south, incognito. Their purpose: to meet and greet, and find out what's happening with both *our* customers and our competitors…and *their* customers.

We now follow up on all of the letters we receive—not just to make sure we have the orders right, but also to identify and track trends…and to collect information on desired products, features, and accessories that we can build into our new toy development process. And we're constantly monitoring our competition to keep up with who's selling what…and how the marketplace appears to be responding to it.

To be sure, the information we collect on our "field trips" is valuable and beneficial. But the *process* of collecting that data has proven to be even more beneficial. It's helped the elves and reindeer understand (better than any training program could convey) that everything we do revolves around customers…and that changing to meet their needs is a good thing. Now employees are actually *recommending* change instead of being "victims" of it and lamenting that the old guy in the red suit can't seem to make up his mind.

Teach "the Business" of the Business

Our experiences both with red wagons and the whole field trip strategy led me to an important conclusion—which has since become a key Santa

leadership principle: **the more employees understand about how the business works, the more
likely they are to accept and support change**.

Having reviewed our employee database, I was
keenly aware that we had very few business or finance
majors on staff. In fact, many of our folks had never
completed any type of basic business course at all.
And those who did had pretty much forgotten what
they had learned. Armed with that knowledge, I
decided to take things to the next level by providing
all the elves and reindeer with in-depth information
and education about how our organization operates
and what's involved in keeping it going.

I started by having our training group develop and
conduct a basic business literacy course through which
everyone would learn concepts like "cash flow," "cost
of goods sold" (in our case, cost of goods *delivered*),
and "first/last in, first out" (FIFO and LIFO).

I then "opened up the books"—giving the staff
more access to financial information such as production costs, overhead expenses, and the like. And
we gave that information true meaning by teaching
the elves and reindeer how to read and interpret

the data…and how to *use* it in the performance of their jobs.

That was followed by instituting regular **State of the Workshop** meetings to keep everyone informed about what's happening (future plans, new products, planned purchases and upgrades, staffing issues, field trip reports, etc.).

A series of brainstorming exercises led to three other highly successful initiatives:

* ❋ Having different elves and reindeer attend, observe, and even participate in nonconfidential senior-staff meetings.

* ❋ Cross-training and rotating assignments within departments so employees can understand and appreciate the functions of, and challenges faced by, their coworkers.

* ❋ A departmental "swap" program that allows individuals to experience how other business units operate…and how we're all interdependent in achieving our overall mission.

For us, teaching "the business" of the business has been *good business*. It's given the elves and reindeer additional opportunities to get involved in what we do, it's helped them grow and develop, and it's produced greater workshop-wide acceptance, support, and understanding of the need for change.

Most importantly, it's made them feel like true "partners" in the running of our North Pole operation…because *THEY ARE!*

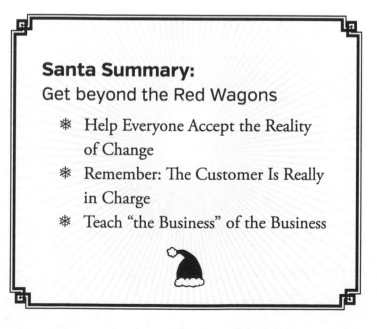

Santa Summary:
Get beyond the Red Wagons

* Help Everyone Accept the Reality of Change
* Remember: The Customer Is Really in Charge
* Teach "the Business" of the Business

SHARE THE MILK AND COOKIES

Help Them See the Difference They Make

One of the biggest benefits of being Santa Claus is the fact that I'm on "the point." Although most everyone works his or her little ears and antlers off to make sure our mission is accomplished, *I'm* the one usually in the spotlight. Who are the zillions of letters we receive each year addressed to? Me. Who gets the credit for the elf-made presents found under all those trees each year? Me. Who enjoys milk and freshly baked cookies in warm homes while the reindeer try to catch their breath on cold rooftops? Me again. And who is the only member of our North Pole team who regularly gets to get out and see, first-hand, the smiles that our work produces? Yep, you guessed it…it's me.

Those benefits (and many more like them) are

a large part of what gets and keeps me motivated. They're great—great, that is, if you happen to be *me*. But, unfortunately, there's only one Santa. And, with the exception of an occasional field trip, most of the elves and reindeer don't get to see and experience the same things that I do. So their feelings of satisfaction and accomplishment must come in different ways— from other sources. As the leader, I play a critical role in making that a reality.

A key strategy I apply in performing that role is to help each elf and reindeer see the positive differences that he or she is making for those we serve… and for each other; I help them see *their* part of the big "making-people-happy" picture.

I start out by spending time with all members of the workshop team discussing how their functions, efforts, and contributions are vital to what we do. It's not unusual for me to pull a box of crayons out of my sack and draw a diagram—showing the physical link between an elf or reindeer (on one side) and a smiling child holding a present (on the other side). Doing that reinforces two messages that I'm constantly communicating to the staff: 1) We don't make and deliver toys, we make and deliver *happiness*, and 2) We couldn't do that without *YOU!*

I make it a priority to spend one-on-one time with each and every elf and reindeer—telling them face-to-face how their individual talents contribute to the team and make a difference to those who will unwrap their handiwork on Christmas morning.

I also make sure that everyone sees the scores of thank-you letters that start coming in around mid-January. I post them on a large board in the workshop that's labeled: *SEE WHAT YOU MADE HAPPEN.* I also post my reply (thank you for the thank-you) letters—which always begin with the words, "On behalf of all the elves and reindeer...." And I often ask members of the staff to write and sign the replies themselves.

Finally, I take a few elves with me on each season's delivery run. When we return, I call a total-team meeting at which my traveling companions and I share our experiences with everyone.

Nothing motivates employees more than knowing they're making a difference. Find ways to make that happen in *your* workshop.

Do Right by Those Who Do Right

I admit it. There was a period, long ago, when I had fallen into the trap of taking my workers for granted. Things were running smoothly. The elves were cranking out quality toys by the thousands. And the reindeer were pulling the sleigh through the midnight sky at what is now called "warp speed." When an occasional problem arose, staff members dealt with it and fixed it. That was, after all, their job…it was what they were expected to do. And as always, I was very busy. So I regularly responded with *NO RESPONSE*. I said and did nothing as long as my expectations were being met.

Then one afternoon, as we were loading the sleigh for our big run, one of the elves asked a very profound question. "Hey boss," he said, "good little girls and boys get all these toys. What do good elves and reindeer get?" Hmmm. I thought about those words all eve long. By the time we returned to the North Pole, I realized that I had failed to apply one of the basic premises of our business to my employees: good performance should be reinforced with positive consequences.

Share the Milk and Cookies

I decided then and there to forget the typical *Elves shouldn't be rewarded for just doing their jobs and I'm too busy to give recognition* rationalizations. I chose to make a change—one that definitely turned out to be for the better…for everyone.

Since that experience, I've worked hard at developing one of the most important characteristics of effective leadership: an "attitude of gratitude." I've learned to truly appreciate workers who meet or exceed my expectations. More importantly, I've learned to *show* that appreciation through my actions and behaviors. I look for, and seize, opportunities to give verbal and written atta-elves (and atta-deers)—opportunities to say *thank you* for doing right.

Now, when someone in the shop does consistently good work for an extended period, or exhibits things like exceptional attendance and conduct, I give him or her the recognition that is due. Whenever individuals or teams go "above and beyond" or make special contributions, I reward them. When staff members display behaviors that support important values like integrity, customer service, teamwork, and responsibility, I commend them. And there's no question that the elves and reindeer appreciate *my* appreciation.

I've learned that recognizing employees—doing right by those who do right—is one of the best things I can do for my elves and reindeer—and for myself as well. *I* feel good when I do it…*they* feel good when they receive it…and they're more motivated, and therefore more likely to repeat the performance I want and need in the future.

Everyone wins. What a deal. It's happy holidays for all!

Expand the Reinforcement Possibilities

Now that I'm a (self-declared) "share the glory and pass the recognition" zealot, I operate by a simple rule of thumb: the more reinforcement of good work, the merrier. But that's not necessarily an easy rule to live by. Why? Because of two misconceptions common in workshops across the land: 1) "There's very little we can do. Money and options are limited." and 2) "Recognition and reinforcement are strictly management activities, and we only have so many managers." Those same beliefs existed here once upon a time—especially in *my* head. And I knew they needed to be overcome. The solution was as clear as an unshaken snow globe: we needed more *things* to do, and more *people* doing them.

We tackled the first misconception with thought and creativity. I worked on my own, and then with my team leaders, to develop a list of low-cost, high-impact ways to recognize our elves and reindeer. We challenged ourselves to come up with as many ideas as possible— ideas that went beyond the typical pat on the back and armed us with different North Pole strokes for different North Pole folks. I was absolutely amazed at how many items we came up with. From letters home to families, to special training and assignments—from prime spots in the employee sleigh lot, to appreciation certificates we printed in the shop—from nominations for our formal awards program, to springing for (you knew it was coming) milk and cookies—the possibilities were and are endless!

Addressing the second misconception— that reinforcing and recognizing good work was management's job alone—proved to be a horse (make that reindeer) of a different color...and a bit more challenging. The task was to get workshop-wide acceptance of the notion that recognition was everyone's job...*everyone's* responsibility. And that meant changing some long-held beliefs and accompanying behaviors.

I started with real workshop examples to help everyone see how we **ALL** benefit from the good work of individual elves, reindeer, and team leaders. Then I asked for a show of hands and hooves of those who regularly praised their coworkers. As expected, the count was very small. When I asked why that was, the most common response was, "That's your job, not ours." I responded with, "Why is that? Who made that rule? Why shouldn't everyone be grateful...and show it?" No one had a good answer. The "why" questions definitely had made the point.

I immediately asked them all to give it a try, and they agreed. I made and distributed a sheet listing ways to recognize and reinforce coworker performance. And I've kept the concept alive by talking about it at staff meetings, doing it myself, and by making sure I give recognition to those who recognize others.

Look for ways to expand the reinforcement possibilities where you work. Make that previously mentioned "attitude of gratitude" one of *your* most important workshop values.

Santa Summary:
Share the Milk and Cookies

* Help Them See the Difference They Make
* Do Right by Those Who Do Right
* Expand the Reinforcement Possibilities

FIND OUT WHO'S NAUGHTY AND NICE

Confront Performance Problems...Early

I don't know about you, but for me, the one aspect of leadership that I find the most difficult and distasteful is dealing with employee performance problems. Don't really care for it. Never have, doubt that I ever will. It can suck the jolly right out of you and turn "Ho Ho's" into "Woe Woe's." But since occasional problems are inevitable, and since it is the leader's job to address them, this is an area that I've really worked on. And I've gotten better—much better at it—primarily through my experiences with one "Igor the Elf."

Igor was one of the original elves here at the Pole when we started this business. I was new to the job—anxious to make my mark on the world and expecting that each employee would perform well... and that I would be liked by everyone, all the time.

I wanted things nice. I liked nice. And when he started, Igor was just that—nice. But things slowly began to change. I noticed that Igor would occasionally start his shift a few minutes late and take longer than scheduled breaks and lunches. My response was *NO* response—which I rationalized with "I'll let it slide because he does good work," and "It's no real problem right now. But if it becomes one, you can bet I'll act." Both of those were code phrases for what I realized deep inside: "I don't have the courage to do what I know needs to be done." So I overlooked Igor's tardiness (Mistake No. 1)—hoping that it would magically go away on its own. Of course, it didn't…it continued. Then, instead of dealing with Igor one-on-one, I chose to send out a memo to the entire workshop staff reminding everyone of the importance of being on time (Mistake No. 2). I hoped Igor would read it, get the message, and correct the problem without my involvement. Of course, he didn't. And all the other elves were left wondering why I sent a reminder about something they already knew and were abiding by.

As the problem continued, I looked for every excuse to avoid a confrontation (Mistake No. 3). But the issue came to a head when one of the other elves approached me and asked, "When are you gonna do something about Igor? His being late all the time is really unfair to the rest of us." The elf was right. I knew I had to do something, and I was furious that Igor had put me in this position. So I called him into my office and unloaded on him (Mistake No. 4). We were both angry and the tension was high. And then *he* asked a question that shut me up faster than a raised eyebrow from Mrs. Claus: "If this issue is so important, why didn't you say something to me sooner?" There was no good answer to offer, only excuses—the same type of excuses I wouldn't accept from others. I *had* been unfair to the other elves... and to Igor as well. I'd seen something I didn't like— something I knew was wrong—and I had failed to do anything about it. I was as much to blame for Igor's continuing problem as he was...and I knew it. I swore, then and there, never to let that happen again. And I haven't. Now I deal with performance problems early and calmly—before they get big.

Coach "the Majority in the Middle"

What do you think about when you gaze at the sky on a clear night? What do you see? For me— especially when I'm driving the sleigh through the heavens on our big delivery run—I see stars…lots of them. And those stars remind me of my elves and reindeer. There are **falling stars** that represent the few employees who exhibit performance problems like Igor, and there are bright novas—the **super stars** that represent the opposite in employee performance—whom I'll discuss in the next section. Most of the lights in the sky, however, are neither falling stars nor supernovas. They're what I call the **middle stars**, and they typify the vast majority of our North Pole employees.

The middle star group is the backbone of our workshop. They're the good, solid workers who, day in, day out, bring our mission to life. And many of them have either positive or negative potential; some have the capacity to experience super-stardom, while others run the risk of slipping into the falling-star ranks.

Obviously, for us to be successful, it's imperative that these middle stars avoid falling backwards. They need to stay as good performers or, better yet, move to the superior-performer level. And as a leader, I play *the* critical role in making that happen. I meet that responsibility by applying various strategies and techniques that fall within the broad management category known as "coaching." Certainly, the term "coaching" means different things to different people. And one could argue that there are almost as many components *to it* as there are people who can benefit *from it*. But, since the older I get the simpler I like things, I've come to define coaching very simply: helping the elves and reindeer avoid problems and do the best work that they can. And doing that with my middle stars includes the following:

❋ Making sure that they know and understand the performance expectations that come with employment.

❋ Providing the training and resources they need to meet those expectations.

❋ Giving frequent and specific feedback on how they're doing.

❋ Identifying any obstacles they may be facing, and then doing my best to eliminate those barriers.

❋ Teaching them how to set, manage, and achieve goals.

❋ Helping them learn from mistakes…and successes.

❋ Partnering with mentors from the super-star ranks.

and, as I learned from the Igor experience...

❋ Staying aware of what they're doing and "nipping in the bud" any problems that start to surface.

When it comes to managing the majority in the middle, the goal is clear: make sure they avoid being naughty, help them stay nice, and work with them to get even "nicer."

Don't Forget "the Super Stars"

Bet you didn't know that I'm a huge sports fan. It's true! I love sporting events of all kinds, and I watch them on television every chance I get (although the reception isn't always so good at the North Pole). I especially enjoy championship games and the Olympics because they involve "the best of the best" athletes—many of whom started in their sport with equipment from us.

Each time I watch, I note a very interesting fact: before, during, and after their events, super stars spend time talking with—and listening to—their coaches. They *ALL* have coaches…and they often credit current and past coaches for helping them become (and continue to be) the superior performers that they are. Why wouldn't they? After all, people don't get to the top of anything all by themselves. And few, if any, *stay* on top without help and guidance from others. That's the essence of coaching… and the essence of this next leadership gift for you.

Your super stars earned their way into that category just like my top elves and reindeer did—by exhibiting consistently outstanding performance. And I used to think that the best thing I could do for those folks was to leave them alone and let them do *their* thing. Boy was I wrong! Like everyone else, great performers don't like to be ignored or taken for granted. Even though some may not admit it publicly, in private most realize that they need to be worked with, involved, recognized, and rewarded. In other words, they need to be coached. But with this group, the coaching role is a little different. For me, it's one of Santa the Encourager, Santa the Developer, and Santa the Cheerleader. And just like with the middle stars, I have several specific techniques I employ. I make a special effort to:

* Get them involved in decision-making, strategy setting, procedure development, and problem solving.
* Delegate extensively and avoid "micromanaging" them.
* Encourage them to teach and mentor others...including me.
* Celebrate their accomplishments and successes.
* Provide them with highly specialized training and other career-growth opportunities.
* Show interest in their work...and their lives away from work.

❋ Hold their coworkers accountable for doing *their* jobs so that the super stars don't have to pick up the slack.

❋ Avoid punishing them for good performance. ("You did such a good job handling that mess, the next time we get one, we'll give it to you again.")

As a leader, the key to dealing with super stars is to demonstrate—through words and actions—that you know and appreciate the fact that they are the *nicest* of "the nice."

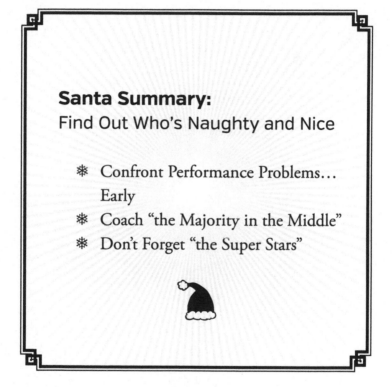

Santa Summary:
Find Out Who's Naughty and Nice

* Confront Performance Problems...
  Early
* Coach "the Majority in the Middle"
* Don't Forget "the Super Stars"

BE GOOD FOR GOODNESS SAKE

Set the Example

If I've learned anything over the many years of wearing this red suit, it's that leadership is *NOT* for the paranoid at heart. Like most managers, I operate in a fish bowl. I'm constantly being watched. The elves are always looking my way to see what I'm doing. And the reindeer get cricks in their necks from checking on what Santa's up to at any given moment. They're all watching…they're all learning. They're learning about what's acceptable behavior here at the top of the world—especially when it comes to matters of ethics and integrity.

Imagine what would happen if we had just one ethics slip at the North Pole…just one time when we failed to do the right thing. It would be disastrous. Our excellent reputation—built over centuries of hard work and attention to detail—could be tarnished (or destroyed entirely) by a single inappropriate act.

How could the customers we serve ever believe in a Santa and crew who broke the rules, cut corners, or failed to meet their commitments? How could all the little ones out there be expected to be good, knowing that Santa Claus isn't? How could anyone even think of writing a "Dear Santa" letter ever again?

The answer is: they couldn't! And that would quickly spell the end of our legend…and our business. That's why ethics is so important to us—that's why making sure that integrity "happens" is one of my most critical responsibilities.

You see, I'm the leader here. And obviously, I have a strong influence on the thoughts and behaviors of the elves and the reindeer. They rightfully assume that it's okay to do whatever *I* do. Regardless of what's said or written elsewhere in the workshop, my actions—whether good or bad—are the performance standards that they will follow.

There's no getting around it: I must model the behaviors that I expect from others. I must take the

LEAD. I must be the first to "walk the talk" when it comes to things like:

* Following *ALL* of our rules and procedures
* Treating *EVERYONE* with dignity and respect
* *ALWAYS* telling the truth
* *NEVER* breaking a promise or commitment
* Building superior quality into *EVERYTHING* I do
* *CONTINUALLY* giving my best effort
* *CONSISTENTLY* taking a stand for what's right

Would you expect anything less from Santa Claus? Probably not. My workers expect nothing less of me either. And *your* people expect the same of *YOU!*

Establish Guidelines & Accountability

Because ethics is so important to us, I can't rely on my example alone for ensuring that everyone does the right thing. Certainly, I do my best to bring on workers who value and demonstrate integrity. And elves, in general, are a pretty ethical bunch to begin with. But they are human (bet you didn't know that), and therefore are susceptible to occasional slips, temptations, and lapses in judgment—as we all are. And, just like the rest of us, they need guidelines, direction, and clear expectations to help them stay on track.

So I make sure that all staff members are well-versed in the laws, rules, and procedures that apply to them. We spend a lot of time discussing—in specific, "how to" terms—what it means to be ethical. And, to help guide their (and my) actions and decisions, we worked together to develop this:

THE WORKSHOP *"What's Right?"* TEST

1. Is it legal?
2. Does it comply with our workshop rules and guidelines?
3. Is it in sync with our North Pole values?
4. Will I be comfortable, guilt-free, or even jolly if I do it?
5. Does it support our goals, commitments, and mission?

6. Would I do it to my family or friends?
7. Would I be perfectly okay with someone doing it to me?
8. Would the most ethical individual I know of do it?

All the guidelines we provide are valuable and important. But for them to have true meaning and really matter, they must be backed with accountabilities and consequences. Just as most children know that failing to be good can result in Santa skipping their house, everyone here at the workshop knows that doing wrong will likely result in a coaching session from Santa…or worse.

For me, building accountability for proper behavior involves the following:

Keeping my eyes and ears open to what's happening.

Through visits, feedback, reports, meetings, etc., I make sure that I'm aware of *what* is being done and how it's being accomplished.

Providing ongoing feedback.

I regularly meet with the elves and reindeer to discuss their performance, share my observations, and reemphasize the importance of integrity-driven workshop practices.

Displaying "zero tolerance."

Ethics violations don't occur very often at the Pole. But when they do, I take swift and deliberate action. I stop the offense, conduct an investigation, and initiate the appropriate consequences.

Think the elves might resent this level of accountability? Well, they don't. They actually support it. Some even demand it. They expect me to take a strong stand in preserving the principles that they take so much pride in having.

Remember That Everything Counts

It was a Friday afternoon. I thought it would be nice to pay a surprise visit to a local mall and let children sit on the *REAL* Santa's lap for a change. After about twenty little ones came and went, Michael took his turn on my knee. "Well Michael," I asked, "have you been a good little boy?" "Yes, I have," he replied. And then he continued, "I've been very good. Maybe I did tell a little lie. And I cheated on a game and called my sister stupid. But those things don't count...do they, Santa?"

How would you have answered Michael? Chances are it would be the same response I offered: "Actually, Michael, those things *do* count. Being good means being good all the time. There are no time-outs...no crossing your fingers behind your back. *Everything* counts." That's the same thing I tell my elves and reindeer, and it's the same advice I offer to you as a leader.

When it comes to our business, we've never broken any laws (at least none that I know about) or fibbed about our finances. I'm guessing that your workshop can make the same claim. Most can. But doing right involves a lot more than avoiding those big "corporate sins." I've learned that it's our day in, day out, seemingly insignificant actions and behaviors that determine our overall goodness. I constantly remind myself of that as I work to set the proper example and hold everyone accountable.

Here at the workshop, we *do* focus on the big integrity issues. But we also give equal, if not more, attention to the "small stuff." I challenge myself and my staff to periodically examine just how ethical we are by looking at...

* The way we treat and talk about each other
* The type of jokes we share
* The little white lies we don't (or do) tell
* The commitments we make and keep (or don't keep)
* The workshop supplies we don't (or do) take home
* The "unimportant" rules we follow (or break)
* The level of quality we put into our toys
* The fact that we don't (or do) use the sleigh for personal business
* The way we respond (or don't respond) to the letters we receive
* The credit we appropriately share (or don't share) with our fellow workers

These, and scores of behaviors like them, reflect who we are here at the Pole and what we stand for. Looking at them helps us to understand and remember that being good and doing right are not *some*time things—they're *every* time things involving everything we do.

EVERYTHING COUNTS—for your people, and especially for *you* as their leader.

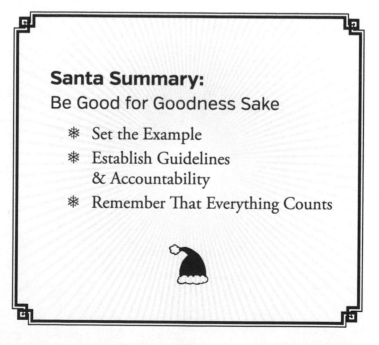

Santa Summary:
Be Good for Goodness Sake

❄ Set the Example
❄ Establish Guidelines
  & Accountability
❄ Remember That Everything Counts

CLOSING THOUGHTS

There's a question that has been pondered for centuries and probably will be debated for years to come:

Is Santa Claus a real person?

Well, *I* think I am. The elves and reindeer think so too. Mrs. Claus certainly believes I exist. And to be sure, somebody had to write this book. But truth be told, whether or not I'm "real" isn't all that important. There are, however, two facts that are *very* important…and very real:

1. To survive and prosper, you and your organization must be able to achieve "big things" throughout each year.
2. You can't get those big things done without effective leadership.

Those are the reasons this book was written… those are why you should pay attention to the information found in this special guide.

You see, **it's not easy being a leader**. Your job comes with many challenges and responsibilities, as you well know. But it is an important and necessary job. And it can be a rewarding one—if you do it right. Helping you do that is precisely what the *Leadership Secrets of Santa Claus* is all about.

With this book, you've been given a valuable gift wrapped in a bunch of good wishes. What you choose to do with it, however, is entirely up to you. As with other holiday presents, you can throw it "in the attic"—never to be seen again, or you can use, appreciate, and enjoy it…and look for ways to pass the favor along to others. Hopefully you'll choose the latter.

There's no question that *your* elves and reindeer are depending on you—just as you depend on them. Don't let them down! Apply the concepts and strategies you've been exposed to within these pages. Take advantage of other resources and opportunities to hone your personal skills. Those are the greatest gifts *you* can give to your people, your organization, and yourself.

Most importantly, never forget that getting big things done all year long isn't about magic. It's about leadership.

Happy holidays. Happy all days!

SUMMARY CHECKLIST

1. Build a Wonderful Workshop
- ❑ Make the Mission the Main Thing
- ❑ Focus on Your People As Well As Your Purpose
- ❑ Let Values Be Your Guide

2. Choose Your Reindeer Wisely
- ❑ Hire Tough So You Can Manage Easy
- ❑ Promote the Right Ones…for the Right Reasons
- ❑ Go for the Diversity Advantage

3. Make a List and Check It Twice
- ❑ Plan Your Work
- ❑ Work Your Plan
- ❑ Make the Most of What You Have

4. Listen to the Elves
- ❑ Open Your Ears to Participation
- ❑ Pay Attention to How You're Perceived
- ❑ Walk Awhile in *Their* Shoes

5. Say Ho Ho Ho, but Don't Forget the Snow
- ❑ Build Contagious Enthusiasm
- ❑ Expect the Unexpected
- ❑ Get Problems Solved…Together

6. Give Them Gifts That Last a Lifetime
- ❑ Teach Success Skills
- ❑ Reinforce Relationships
- ❑ Push Pride and Professionalism

7. Get beyond the Red Wagons
- ❑ Help Everyone Accept the Reality of Change
- ❑ Remember: The Customer Is Really in Charge
- ❑ Teach "the Business" of the Business

8. Share the Milk and Cookies

- ❑ Help Them See the Difference They Make
- ❑ Do Right by Those Who Do Right
- ❑ Expand the Reinforcement Possibilities

9. Find Out Who's Naughty and Nice

- ❑ Confront Performance Problems…Early
- ❑ Coach "the Majority in the Middle"
- ❑ Don't Forget "the Super Stars"

10. Be Good for Goodness Sake

- ❑ Set the Example
- ❑ Establish Guidelines & Accountability
- ❑ Remember That Everything Counts

REINDEER FOOD FOR THOUGHT

On a scale of 1-10 how "wonderful" is the workshop you are responsible for?

| 1. | 2. | 3. | 4. | 5. | 6. | 7. | 8. | 9. | 10. |

Santa would be disappointed *We're doing pretty well* *Santa would be proud of us*

Based upon your learning about "Santa's leadership secrets," what are some of the positive things you can do more of, less of, and differently in your "workshop"?

More of...

....

....

Less of ....

....

....

Differently ....

....

....

Reindeer Food for Thought

What can you do to help others in your organization apply the "Leadership Secrets of Santa Claus"?

....

....

....

....

....

....

....

....

....

....

....

....

....

....

....

....

....

....

YOUR COMMITMENT LETTER... TO SANTA CLAUS

Dear Santa:

Thank you for sharing your "Leadership Secrets" with me. In response to this wonderful gift, I acknowledge my responsibility to be the best leader that I can possibly be. Toward that end, I commit to rereading this book often and to applying the following techniques and strategies—found within these pages:

_____

_____

_____

_____

    Rather than mailing this letter to you, Santa, I will leave it here—as a personal reminder of the promises I'm making to myself and to the people I lead.

    Thanks for helping me get big things done...all year long!

_____   _____
(Signature)   (Date)

SANTA CLAUSES
WORDS TO REMEMBER

People need me—they depend on me. We're doing something important here. And knowing that gives me the energy to carry the sack, lead the pack, and keep coming back.

PAGE XIV

Just how do I keep everyone, including myself, on track and motivated throughout each year— all for one long night's big splash? The answer is basic and simple: through an unwavering and uncompromising focus on OUR MISSION.

PAGE 2

You can't possibly focus on your mission without also focusing on the folks that make your mission happen.

PAGES 3–4

...it seems to me that what makes a workshop wonderful is not walls and ceilings, but what happens inside those walls and under those ceilings...it's not how a workshop stands, but what it stands for that makes it special.

PAGE 8

Making sure that everyone knows what values are important, and then helping everyone turn those good beliefs into everyday behaviors is how leaders create a great place to work.

PAGES 8–9

The time I spend hiring the right way is nothing compared to the time I'll have to spend dealing with the wrong reindeer.

PAGE 13

It didn't take long to discover that our "different" toy makers came bearing gifts. They brought new skills, perspectives, and ideas to the workshop. They gave us more than one way of thinking, planning, producing, and problem solving. They made us better, stronger, and much more in touch with the "different" shapes, sizes, and colors of customers that we serve.

PAGE 18

Our success—and resulting reputation for excellence—is the result of clearly defined goals combined with well-thought out plans to accomplish those goals.

PAGE 21

Our goals are specific yet flexible—allowing for changing conditions and circumstances. And because staff "buy-in" and commitment are so important to achieving our objectives, I make sure that everyone has input in the goal-setting process.

PAGE 22

Once a reasonable plan is made, we immediately implement it... We get things going fast, and then we make midcourse corrections as necessary. And the way we know how we're doing, as well as what adjustments we need to make, is through continual monitoring and measurement.

PAGES 24–25

...we'd quickly go out of business if we didn't make the absolute best use of our resources: time, money, materials, and the talents of our elves and reindeer.

PAGE 27

...involving workers in running the operation–and in making decisions that affect them–is a key strategy for leadership success.

PAGE 33

I pay attention to what my elves [and others] feel. Perceptions are realities for those that hold them... and I must deal with those realities in order to lead effectively.

PAGE 35

To truly build a workshop that is filled with positive energy, I not only need to set the example individually, but also make the goal of recognizing positive performance part of EVERY reindeer and elf 's job expectations.

PAGE 42

SANTA CLAUSES

Expect the unexpected because all the positive workplace energy you can create cannot help you totally avoid the inevitable obstacles to workshop success.

PAGE 44

Ho Ho Ho's are great for immediate effects, but even more importantly, they're vital for establishing a workshop culture that is built on pride, professionalism, and individual commitment.

PAGE 48

Developing our team is more than just teaching folks how to do their jobs; it's also about teaching them how to be successful.

PAGES 51–52

Occasional squabbles between workers are inevitable. Most workers need help resolving those squabbles. It's my job, as their leader, to help them repair what's broken.

PAGE 55

LEADERSHIP SECRETS OF SANTA CLAUS

When our activities are geared toward helping our employees learn, grow, and develop the work habits of success, we're giving those who rely on us gifts which will serve them well throughout their careers...gifts that last a lifetime.

PAGE 58

I knew we had to abandon the status quo. And as the leader, I had to make it happen with both decisiveness and sensitivity.

PAGE 64

Obviously, our job is to give people what they're looking for. And as their wants and needs change, we have to change along with them. Doing that starts with accepting the fact that the customer is truly in charge of our business...

PAGE 67

The more employees understand about how the business works, the more likely they are to accept and support change.

PAGE 69

SANTA CLAUSES

Nothing motivates employees more than knowing they're making a difference.

PAGE 75

I've learned that recognizing employees—doing right by those who do right—is one of the best things I can do for my elves and reindeer— and for myself as well.

PAGE 78

...for us to be successful, it's imperative that [the] middle stars avoid falling backwards. They need to stay as good performers or, better yet, move to the superior-performer level. And as a leader, I play the critical role in making that happen.

PAGE 87

Like everyone else, great performers don't like to be ignored or taken for granted. Even though some may not admit it publicly, in private most realize that they need to be worked with, involved, recognized, and rewarded. In other words, they need to be coached.

PAGES 90–91

Avoid punishing [super stars] for good performance. ["You did such a good job handling that mess, the next time we get one, we'll give it to you again."]

PAGE 92

You see, I'm the leader here. And obviously, I have a strong influence on the thoughts and behaviors of the elves and reindeer. They rightfully assume that it's okay to do whatever I do. Regardless of what's said or written elsewhere in the workshop, my actions—whether good or bad—are the performance standards that they will follow.

PAGE 96

There's no getting around it: I must model the behaviors that I expect from others. I must take the LEAD. I must be the first to "walk the talk"...

PAGES 96–97

I make sure that all staff members are well-versed in the laws, rules, and procedures

*that apply to them. We spend a lot of time
discussing—in specific, "how to" terms—
what it means to be ethical.*

PAGE 98

*All the guidelines we provide are valuable and
important. But for them to have true meaning
and really matter, they must be backed with
accountabilities and consequences.*

PAGE 99

*Being good means being good all the time.
There are no time-outs...no crossing
your fingers behind your back.*
Everything *counts.*

PAGE 101

*To survive and prosper, you and your organization
must be able to achieve "big things" throughout
each year... You can't get those big things done
without effective leadership.*

PAGE 105

LEADERSHIP SECRETS OF SANTA CLAUS

Your job comes with many challenges and responsibilities, as you well know. But it is an important and necessary job. And it can be a rewarding one—if you do it right.

PAGE 106

...your elves and reindeer are depending on you— just as you depend on them. Don't let them down!

PAGE 106

...never forget that getting big things done all year long isn't about magic. It's about leadership.

PAGE 107

ABOUT THE AUTHOR

Eric Harvey is founder and president of The Walk the Talk Company and a leading expert on high-achieving leaders and organizations. Since its founding in 1977, Walk The Talk has worked with thousands of organizations worldwide including multinational corporations, leading health care providers, high-tech start-ups, and highly respected nonprofit organizations. Eric has authored twenty-five books that have sold millions of copies including the bestsellers: *Walk the Talk, Ethics 4 Everyone, Walk Awhile in My Shoes,* and *Go for the Gold.* He and his wife, Nancy, live in Pensacola Beach, Florida, and are the proud parents of two daughters and six grandchildren.

Please let me know if you have any questions about Santa's Leadership Secrets or would like to give me some feedback about this book. I'd very much appreciate hearing from you.

Best Wishes,
Santa Claus

Santa@walkthetalk.com

MORE
LEADERSHIP TOOLS
FOR YOUR STOCKING

The Leadership Secrets of Santa Claus Workbook

Put your ideas into action with the companion to this book, *The Leadership Secrets of Santa Claus Workbook*! Including thought-provoking tools about how to build your own wonderful workshop, it can be used as a self-study guide or as a component of a facilitator-led development program. The workbook provides an invaluable resource for leaders at all levels to apply their learning directly to their own jobs.

The Leadership Secrets of Santa Claus (gift book version)

One of the most powerful and entertaining business books today, *The Leadership Secrets of Santa Claus* is now available in a gift edition. Elegantly designed and filled with clever, compelling leadership messages, the gift version is for everyone with current leadership responsibilities or future leadership aspirations. It makes a great gift for leaders at all levels or a perfect addition to your personal leadership library.

Visit simpletruths.com for ordering information.